Alice Pa

Champion of Women's Rights

By Linda J. Barth

Published by Amazon Kindle Digital, 2019

This book is dedicated to the suffragists, women and men, who fought so hard to give us the vote and to those who continue to fight for the Equal Rights Amendment.

Published by Amazon Kindle Digital, 2019

Table of Contents

Chapter 1 — The Young Alice

Who would have thought that a quiet **Quaker** girl from South Jersey would one day change the world?

When Alice Stokes Paul was born in Mount Laurel, New Jersey in 1885, only men were allowed to vote in most parts of the United States. Raised in the Quaker religion, Alice believed in "ordinary equality" for all people. Her religion taught her to try to correct injustice in the world, and she saw the voting issue as a major injustice.

Born on January 11, 1885, Alice was soon joined by her brother William, born in 1886, sister Helen (1889), and brother Parry (1895).

Alice and her brother Billy (photo left)

Alice, age 6, and Billy, age 4

As a student at the Friends (Quaker) School in nearby Moorestown, New Jersey, Alice was an avid reader. She once said, "I read just endlessly, ceaselessly, almost every book it seems! I took out every book in the library." She read over and over every single line written by the British author Charles Dickens.

Although quiet and shy by nature, Alice enjoyed playing field hockey, tennis, basketball, and baseball. Her schoolmates said that she was one of the best batters on the team.

While her neighbors rode to school in their family carriages, Alice made the mile-long journey riding her horse bareback.

Old Elementary School - before 1918

Moorestown (NJ) Friends Elementary School.

Built in 1830 - Razed 1933
Friends H.S. 2nd + Chester

Top and bottom: Moorestown Friends High School, which Alice attended.

Built 1830 - Razed 1933

FRIENDS HIGH SCHOOL - Second Street and Chester Avenue, Moorestown, New Jersey   Prior 1920

Chapter 2 — Swarthmore College

She was honored to give the valedictory speech at her high school graduation in 1901 and won a $150 scholarship to attend Swarthmore College.

Alice's mother Tacie had attended Swarthmore too. The school had 100 rules for good behavior. Some of them were: Boys and girls "shall not walk together on the grounds of the College, nor in the neighborhood, nor to and from the railroad station. They shall not coast upon the same sled."

Despite her love of literature, Alice chose to major in science, most unusual for a woman at that time. She explained her reason: "It's the one thing I don't know anything about and I never would read and I can't understand it or comprehend it or have any interest in it are all the things in the field of science."

Alice (seated, right) and her sorority sisters at Swarthmore College

She took biology, chemistry, and math, plus Bible and French. She also studied **elocution** for the same reason she chose science: she might not like it, but she wanted to master it.

Chapter 3 — First Job

After her 1905 graduation from Swarthmore with a degree in biology, Alice moved to New York City to become a **social worker**. She worked at a **settlement house** on Rivington Street in Manhattan's Lower East Side (photo).

There she helped young women and immigrants to form a labor union and ran sewing and gymnasium clubs for people in the neighborhood.

At the same time she took classes and studied at the **New York School of Philanthropy.** Alice and her friends visited theaters and the Metropolitan Museum of Art. They toured Staten Island and Chinatown, activities far removed from her Quaker upbringing. In a letter to her cousin Susannah Parry, she remarked, "I've never been happier in my life."

Although not yet active in politics, Alice was horrified to read about the arrest of sixty British **suffragettes (the British term)** in February 1907. (See photo next page.)

She and her mother found it unacceptable that in 1870 black men in the United States were given the vote, and yet both white and black women still waited for that same right.

(For more about this subject, see the notes at the end of the book.)

Alice soon realized, however, that helping individual poor families was not the best way to bring about change for all people. For one year she studied at the University of Pennsylvania (Penn), earning a master's degree in **sociology** and a minor in political science and economics.

Emmeline Pankhurst is arrested in England during a protest for woman's suffrage.

Chapter 4 — Alice Goes to Europe

In June of 1907 Alice finished her studies at Penn and sailed to Europe "to see something of the world." While living in Berlin, Germany, she studied the German language and sat in on classes at the University of Berlin, which, she discovered, refused to officially admit women to the school.

Returning to England, Alice studied next at Woodbrooke, a Quaker school in Birmingham. While taking a class at the University of Birmingham, Alice attended a lecture by Christabel Pankhurst, the militant English **suffragette.** Pankhurst was shouted down by students who sang, yelled, and whistled throughout her lecture. The university apologized and invited her back. On her second visit, the male students listened silently, and Alice could hear every word of Christabel's speech.

It was then that Alice Paul realized what she had to do.

Christabel Pankhurst

In 1908 Alice learned about two parades in London for women's suffrage: one organized by Christabel Pankhurst's Women's Social and Political Union (WPSU) and the other planned by a less militant group, the National Union of Women's Suffrage Societies (NUWSS). She decided to march in both!

On June 13, thousands of women with colorful red-and-white banners marched calmly for two miles through the streets of London to the Royal Albert Hall for a celebration.

A week later, on June 21, the Pankhursts (mother Emmeline and her three daughters) had organized *seven* processions, each from a different direction, to meet at Hyde Park. The thirty thousand marchers with their white, purple, and green banners, ribbons, sashes, and flags then moved to twenty platforms around the park and heard fiery speeches. At the end, they all shouted, "Votes for Women! Votes for Women! Votes for Women!"

(Christabel had been the first suffragette to go to jail for the cause of women's votes.)

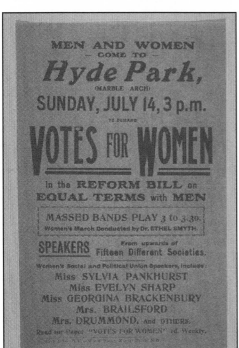

Poster (left) from a similar protest rally in July.

Announcement (below) for the July 21 march

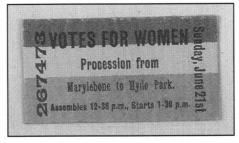

Alice joined the WPSU and followed the motto, "Deeds, not words." She was arrested ten times in England for protesting for women's suffrage. Imprisoned three times in London, she had to endure **forced feedings** during **hunger strikes**.

Perhaps during these hard times, Alice remembered her father's words, "Well, when there is a job to be done, I bank on Alice."

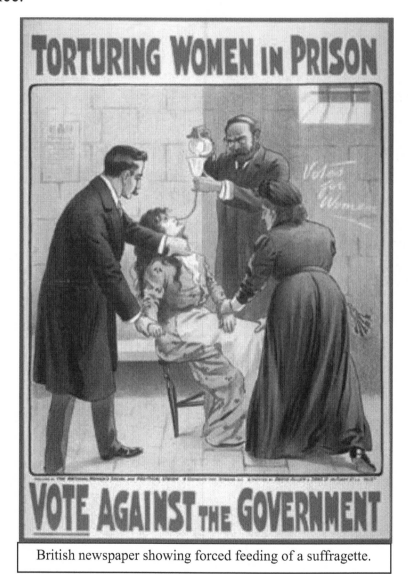

British newspaper showing forced feeding of a suffragette.

Chapter 5 — Return to the United States and Protests in Washington, D.C.

When Alice returned to the United States in 1910, she was invited to join the National American Woman Suffrage Association (NAWSA). At this time, women could vote in some states, but not in <u>all</u> states. NAWSA wanted women to be given the vote one state at a time.

Alice and many other suffragists wanted Congress to pass the 19th Amendment (called the **Susan B. Anthony** amendment) to the Constitution. This change would allow women to vote <u>in all of the states</u>. Because her goals were different from NAWSA's, Alice and others formed a separate group, the National Woman's Party (NWP). But the women still had to convince the new president, Woodrow Wilson, to agree with them.

Anita Pollitzer and Alice Paul at the grave of 19th century suffragist Susan B. Anthony in Rochester, New York

While in England, Alice had learned many tactics for reaching her goal. One of those new ideas was organizing large parades. President Wilson was going to be inaugurated on March 4, 1913. While the eyes of the country were on Washington, DC, Alice planned a parade there on March 3, the day before the inauguration, to convince Wilson to give women the vote.

Photo above shows suffragists on a bus in New York City, part of the hike to Washington, D.C. to join the March 3, 1913 National American Woman Suffrage Association parade. (Times, Feb. 11, 1913)

Thousands of women and men decided to go to Washington for the March 3 parade. This group from New York City rode and hiked to get there on time.

Alice and the other members of the National Woman's Party wrote to women's groups around the country, inviting them to take part in the parade.

They organized 26 floats, ten bands, six chariots, and 8000 women to march for voting rights.

At 3:25 p.m. the parade began with Inez Milholland, the beautiful lawyer and activist, leading the procession. She was dressed in a white suit and boots and sitting astride a white horse.

Inez Milholland leading the parade.

Photo shows float representing Australia at the Woman Suffrage Parade held in Washington, D.C., March 3, 1913.

Photo taken at the Woman Suffrage Parade held in Washington, D.C., March 3, 1913 showing a float with banner "Women of the Bible Lands" passing the U.S. Capitol.

Alice marched in cap and gown. The first float, called "The Great Demand," held this sign:

"We demand an amendment to the United States Constitution enfranchising the women of the country."

The event turned ugly, however, when scores of men who were watching the parade moved in so close that the marchers could barely move forward. Some attacked the suffragists, first with insults and cursing and then with physical violence. The police stood by and watched. Eventually the police chief called the cavalry, which crossed the Potomac and arrived at the parade at 4:30 p.m.

The next day Alice's group of suffragists made headlines across the nation as newspapers carried descriptions of the parade. Suffrage became a topic of discussion among the public and politicians alike.

But the women still had to convince President Woodrow Wilson (below) to agree with them. Two weeks after the parade, Alice and other suffragists met with the President, asking him to support the 19th Amendment, but he was not interested. The women decided to have more parades and rallies.

Chapter 6 — More Protests and Prison Time

Four years went by as the suffragists continued to have rallies around the country. Still President Wilson would not change his mind. At this time, World War I had begun in Europe. The President wanted peace in Europe and did not want to send American soldiers to fight in the war. Alice told the President that if women could vote, they would most likely vote for peace, not war.

Alice had a talent for getting people to try new tactics to reach their goal. Since she worked hard and never complained, the other women worked hard too, following her example.

On January 10, 1917, as the President began his second term in office, Alice directed her members to **picket** on the sidewalk in front of the White House. They carried purple, white, and gold banners and took turns standing there silently every day except Sundays, day and night, in all seasons and weather.

These women were called "silent sentinels" because they stood still like sentinels, or guards, not speaking or arguing with anyone who stopped by. Their banners had messages like this one:

Women prepare to march to the White House to picket.

In June numerous picketers were falsely arrested for blocking traffic. They were sentenced to three days in jail or a $25 fine. All chose jail.

The NWP headquarters was near the White House. When protesters were jailed, others walked to the White House and took their places on the sidewalk.

Then, in mid-July, sixteen women were arrested and sentenced to sixty days in the Occoquan Workhouse in Virginia. This was a horrible place where the prisoners were given spoiled food with worms. They were beaten by guards and forced to stand outside in the cold and rain. The women who became ill were not given medical care.

In late October 1917 Alice was sent to the district jail, having written to her mother that it "will merely be a delightful rest." But she knew it wouldn't be.

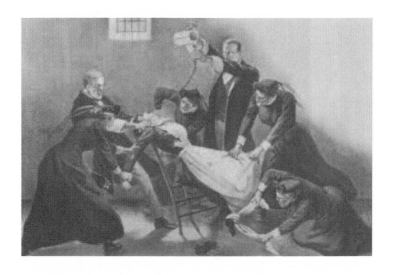

Rats fought with each other and scampered across the floor. Bed bugs covered the hard mattresses that lay upon steel cots.

Alice began a **hunger strike**, refusing to eat. To make her stop the strike, the prison guards would not let her have visitors or messages. Still she would not eat. To keep her alive, the guards and nurses forced her to eat by tying her down, forcing her mouth open, and pouring liquid food through a tube into her nose. This **force feeding**, which

(continued on page 23)

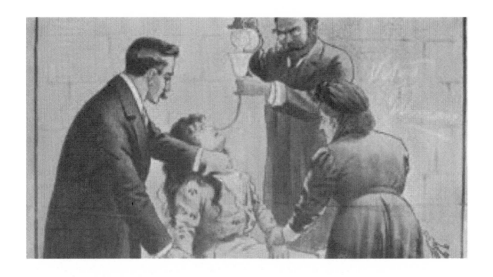

LUCY BURNS

Lucy Burns helped Alice to establish the first permanent headquarters for suffrage work in Washington, D.C. Together they organized the suffrage parade of March 3, 1913. She was one of the editors of *The Suffragist*, led most of the picket demonstrations, and served more time in jail than any other suffragist in America. She was arrested for picketing June 1917 and sentenced to 3 days; arrested September 1917, sentenced to 60 days; arrested November 10, 1917, sentenced to 6 months; in January 1919 arrested at watchfire demonstrations, for which she served one three-day and two five-day sentences. She also served four prison terms in England.

Lucy Burns was one of the speakers on the **"Prison Special"** tour from February to March 1919.

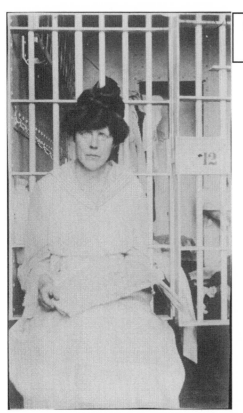

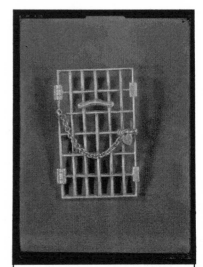

Suffragist Lucy Burns at Occoquan Workhouse

Jail door pin designed by Alice Paul.

Below: Suffragist Lucy Branham in her Occoquan prison dress speaks to the crowd at a stop on the **"Prison Special"** train tour.

was done three times a day, was very painful and caused her to become quite ill.

In November thirty-three women were sent to Occoquan, where they demanded to be treated as political prisoners. This would mean that they could receive mail, visitors, and gifts, wear their own clothing, and read books. Instead, they were dragged and beaten and taken to filthy, dark, damp, cold cells. After eight days of another hunger strike and forced feedings, their lawyer convinced the court to free all of the women, including Alice.

Finally, in January 1918, President Wilson suddenly changed his mind and agreed to the idea of women voting. The very next day, the members of the House of Representatives voted and, by <u>one</u> vote, the 19th Amendment passed. But still, not enough members of the Senate agreed, and the vote there failed.

More parades, marches, arrests, and jailings followed. Then, more than a year later, on May 20, 1919, the House of Representatives again voted in favor of the Susan B. Anthony amendment. Two weeks later, on June 4, 1919 the Senate also approved the amendment.

But the fight was not over. In order for the amendment to become law, three-fourths (3/4) of the state legislatures had to approve. That meant that Alice and the other women had to convince <u>36 state legislatures</u> to approve the 19th Amendment. If that happened before

Alice on the phone to her fellow suffragists to rally support in state legislatures.

November, then women could vote in the 1920 presidential election.

The suffragists set up offices in all of the states, talking to governors and legislators and asking them to approve the 19th Amendment. Slowly the states voted, some for and some against.

Finally, by August 1920, thirty-five states had voted for the suffrage amendment. The Tennessee state legislature could be the thirty-sixth! The first vote ended in a tie, but when the second vote began, the result was still uncertain. Rep. Harry Burn's mother had written to her son, "Hurrah and vote for suffrage and don't keep them in doubt." As a good son, Harry listened to his mother and voted "yes" to break the tie.

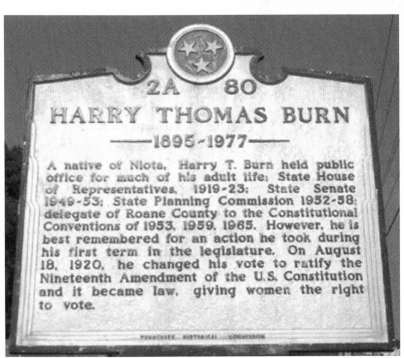

2A   80

HARRY THOMAS BURN
——1895-1977——

A native of Niota, Harry T. Burn held public office for much of his adult life: State House of Representatives, 1919-23; State Senate 1949-53; State Planning Commission 1952-58; delegate of Roane County to the Constitutional Conventions of 1953, 1959, 1965. However, he is best remembered for an action he took during his first term in the legislature. On August 18, 1920, he changed his vote to ratify the Nineteenth Amendment of the U.S. Constitution and it became law, giving women the right to vote.

TENNESSEE HISTORICAL COMMISSION

The Nineteenth Amendment had finally been approved.

Chapter 7 — Victory at Last

Before the November 1920 presidential election, Alice had filed an absentee ballot. This allowed her to vote by mail instead of traveling home to New Jersey. Her signature on the ballot was witnessed by a fellow suffragist, Catherine Flanagan, one of the first female **notaries** appointed after the 19th Amendment was passed.

Alice's mother had started a scrapbook of stories and photographs about her famous daughter. One entry said, "During the summer Suffrage was granted to women & we voted for the first time for the President Nov. 1920. Alice at last saw her dream realized."

Knowing that she needed to understand the law, Alice enrolled at both the George Washington University School of Law and the Washington College School of Law.

She attended one during the day and the other in the evening. She received a law degree from the Washington College of Law in 1922 and master's and doctor's degrees from American University in 1927 and 1928, respectively. Within ten years she had earned three law degrees. Now she was prepared to continue her activities on behalf of equal rights for women.

Chapter 8 — The Equal Rights Amendment

Alice Paul was not through making changes for women. In 1923 she proposed and wrote another amendment, the Equal Rights Amendment (ERA). Voting was not enough, she reasoned. She wanted women to be able to serve on juries, have rights concerning their children, and be allowed to own property.

The main section of the Equal Rights Amendment reads, "Equality of rights under the law shall not be denied or abridged by the United States or by any state on account of sex."

Many women's groups opposed the ERA because they thought it might take away the few rights women already had. They argued that working women needed to keep the special protections they had concerning working conditions, wages, and hours.

In 1972, the ERA was finally passed by Congress and sent to the states for ratification. The original seven-year time limit was extended by Congress to June 30, 1982, but by that deadline, the ERA had been ratified by only 35 states, three short of the 38 required to put it into the Constitution.

On March 22, 2017, Nevada became the 36th state to ratify the Equal Rights Amendment, followed by Illinois on May 30, 2018. A subcommittee in the Virginia legislature did not approve the amendment in January 2019.

When the 38th state passes the ERA, supporters will ask Congress to pass a statute proclaiming that the measure has been approved by thirty-eight states. If that happens, the ERA will become law.

Alice Paul died on July 9, 1977, having fought until the end for the passage of the Equal Rights Amendment.

Her home, Paulsdale, is now the headquarters of the Alice Paul Institute, which teaches about the life and work of Alice Stokes Paul and offers girls' leadership programs.

The mission of the Alice Paul Institute is to honor the legacy of Alice Paul's work for gender equality through education and leadership development.

Its vision statement is "Gender equality for all." The Alice Paul Institute reminds us that Alice Paul led the final fight to get women the vote and wrote the Equal Rights Amendment. They honor her legacy as a role model of leadership in the continuing quest for equality.

Paulsdale is a National Historic Landmark, located at 128 Hooten Road, Mount Laurel, New Jersey. You can learn more at www.alicepaul.org.

"I never doubted that equal rights was the right direction. Most reforms, most problems are complicated. But to me there is nothing complicated about ordinary equality."

– Alice Paul, 1974

State Legislatures and the Equal Rights Amendment

States that <u>have</u> ratified the Equal Rights Amendment

Alaska	Iowa	Nebraska	Pennsylvania
California	Kansas	Nevada	Rhode Island
Colorado	Kentucky	New Hampshire	South Dakota
Connecticut	Maine	New Jersey	Tennessee
Delaware	Maryland	New Mexico	Texas
Hawaii	Massachusetts	New York	Vermont
Idaho	Michigan	North Dakota	Washington
Illinois	Minnesota	Ohio	West Virginia
Indiana	Montana	Oregon	Wisconsin
			Wyoming

States that <u>have not</u> ratified the Equal Rights Amendment

Alabama	Mississippi
Arizona	Missouri
Arkansas	North Carolina
Florida	Oklahoma
Georgia	South Carolina
Louisiana	Utah

From the website: https://www.equalrightsamendment.org/

What is the complete text of the Equal Rights Amendment?

Section 1: Equality of rights under the law shall not be denied or abridged by the United States or by any state on account of sex.
Section 2: The Congress shall have the power to enforce, by appropriate legislation, the provisions of this article.
Section 3: This amendment shall take effect two years after the date of ratification.

This wording has been the text of the Equal Rights Amendment since it was composed by suffragist leader and women's rights activist Alice Paul in 1923. The original ERA, written in 1923 by Paul, feminist lawyer/activist Crystal Eastman, and several others was known as the "Lucretia Mott Amendment": "Men and women shall have equal rights throughout the United States and every place subject to its jurisdiction. Congress shall have power to enforce this article by appropriate legislation."

Beginning in the 113th Congress (2014-2015), the text of the ERA ratification bill introduced in the House of Representatives has differed slightly from both the traditional wording and its Senate companion bill. It reads:
Section 1: Women shall have equal rights in the United States and every place subject to its jurisdiction. Equality of rights under the law shall not be denied or abridged by the United States or by any State on account of sex.
Section 2: Congress and the several States shall have the power to enforce, by appropriate legislation, the provisions of this article.
Section 3: This amendment shall take effect two years after the date of ratification.

The addition of the first sentence specifically names women in the Constitution for the first time and clarifies the intent of the amendment to make discrimination on the basis of a person's sex unconstitutional. The addition of "and the several States" in Section 2 restores wording that was drafted by Alice Paul but removed before the amendment's 1972 passage. It affirms that enforcement of the constitutional prohibition of sex discrimination is a function of both federal and state levels of government.

Chapter 9 — The Belmont-Paul Women's Equality National Monument

In April 2016 the National Park Service designated as a historic site the Belmont-Paul Women's Equality National Monument, the home that served as the National Woman's Party headquarters in Washington, D.C.

It was from this headquarters that Alice Paul and Alva Belmont organized the picketing at the White House that ultimately led to the passage of the 19th Amendment.

This historic home is located at 144 Constitution Ave NE in Washington, DC. You may learn more at www.nps.gov/bepa/.

Chapter 10 — Women's Suffrage Around the World

In many other countries, women won the right to vote before those in America. In other nations, women won the vote much more recently.

1893 New Zealand
1902 Australia[1]
1906 Finland
1913 Norway
1915 Denmark
1917 Canada[2]
1918 Austria, Germany, Poland, Russia
1919 Netherlands
1920 United States
1921 Sweden
1928 Britain, Ireland
1931 Spain
1934 Turkey
1944 France
1945 Italy
1947 Argentina, Japan, Mexico, Pakistan
1949 China
1950 India
1954 Colombia
1957 Malaysia, Zimbabwe
1962 Algeria
1963 Iran, Morocco
1964 Libya
1967 Ecuador

1971 Switzerland
1972 Bangladesh
1974 Jordan
1976 Portugal
1989 Namibia
1990 Western Samoa
1993 Kazakhstan, Moldova
1994 South Africa
2005 Kuwait
2006 United Arab Emirates
2011 Saudi Arabia[3]

NOTE: One country does not allow their people, male or female, to vote: Brunei.

1. Australian women, with the exception of aboriginal women, won the vote in 1902. Aborigines, male and female, did not have the right to vote until 1962.

2. Canadian women, with the exception of Canadian Indian women, won the vote in 1917. Canadian Indians, male and female, did not win the vote until 1960. *Source: The New York Times,* May 22, 2005.

3. King Abdullah of Saudi Arabia issued a decree in 2011 ordering that women be allowed to stand as candidates and vote in municipal elections, but their first opportunity did not come until Dec. 2015, almost a year after the king's death in January of that year.

GLOSSARY

Anthony, Susan B. —Susan B. Anthony (1820-1906) was a suffragist, abolitionist, author, and speaker who was the president of the National American Woman Suffrage Association. a suffragist, abolitionist, author and speaker who was the president of the National American Woman Suffrage Association.

Elocution—the art of public speaking

Forced feeding—a practice of some prisons to force nourishment into prisoners who were on a hunger strike and refused to eat.

Hunger strike—the act of refusing to eat as a way of showing that you strongly disagree with or disapprove of something.

New York School of Philanthropy—the first higher education program to train people who wanted to work in the field of charity in the United States. Established in 1898.

Notary—a public officer who certifies or witnesses writings and signatures to make them authentic and takes affidavits and depositions.

Pankhurst, Christabel—Together with her mother Emmeline and sister Sylvia, Christabel Pankhurst was one of the leaders of the women's suffrage movement in Britain, fighting for votes for women. Emmeline and Christabel were the founders of the Women's Social and Political Union, directing a campaign that included massed rallies, hunger strikes, and physical action. Christabel was the first suffragist to go to jail for the cause of women's votes.

Picket—to stand or march in a public place in order to protest something.

"Prison Special" Tour —a three-week train tour in February 1919 in which twenty-six members of the National Woman's Party stopped in cities to describe the inhumane prison sentences served by so many women who fought for the vote.

Quaker—a member of a Christian sect that stresses Inner Light, rejects sacraments and an ordained ministry, and opposes war; also called the Society of Friends.

Settlement house—a place or organization that provides various community services to people in a crowded part of a city. American settlements were in neighborhoods populated by recent European immigrants, few of whom spoke English. The houses had gymnasiums, auditoriums, classrooms, and meeting halls, as well as living space and dining facilities for a dozen or more residents.

Social worker—someone who works for a government or private organization that helps people who have financial or family problems.

Sociology—the science of society, social institutions, and social relationships; *specifically*: the systematic study of the development, structure, interaction, and collective behavior of organized groups of human beings.

Suffragettes—People (mainly women) in Great Britain who worked to get voting rights for women.

Suffragists—people (mainly women) who worked to get voting rights for women. This term is more often used in the United States.

BACK NOTES

Even though the suffragists were clubbed and beaten, Alice Paul never allowed her marchers to retaliate. These nonviolent tactics of civil disobedience that Alice Paul promoted were used later by Martin Luther King Jr. during the civil rights protests of the 1960s and by those protesting against the Vietnam War in the 1970s.

On March 30, 1870 the 15th Amendment to the Constitution was passed. It read, "The right of citizens of the United States to vote shall not be denied or abridged by the United States or by any State on account of race, color, or previous condition of servitude." **This statement, however, did not apply to women. It permitted black men to vote.**

As a side note, the day after that amendment became law, on March 31, 1870, the City of Perth Amboy, New Jersey held an election to determine whether the city charter should be revised or whether the city should become a township. Several people reminded Thomas Mundy Peterson, a former slave, that he was now allowed to vote, so he went home, had lunch, walked to the polling place, and voted.

It took forty more years for the nation to approve the 19th Amendment.

Acknowledgements

Alice Paul Institute: Lucienne Beard, Kris Myers, Lee Ann Vozdivic, Jacqueline Burke
Alisa Dupuy, historical interpreter.

Photographs courtesy of the Alice Paul Institute, the Library of Congress, the Museum of London, Moorestown Friends School, and the Belmont-Paul Women's Equality National Monument. Photo of Harry Burn courtesy of Tennessee State Library and Archives, Calvert Brothers Studio Glass Plate Negatives Collection.

Sources
The Alice Paul Institute, 128 Hooten Road, Mount Laurel, New Jersey 08054.

Berkeley University, Suffragist Oral History Project. http://bancroft.berkeley.edu/ROHO/projects/suffragist/

Herendeen, Anne. "What the Home Town Thinks of Alice Paul." Everybody's Magazine, 1919, Vol. 41, 4.
Transcribed by Trista di Genova, trista@womensparty.com, 3/02

Raum, Alice. *Alice Paul*. American Lives series. Heinemann Library, Chicago, 2004.

Sagan, Miriam. *Women's Suffrage*. Lucent Books, San Diego, California, 1995.

Zahniser, J.D. and Amelia R. Fry. *Alice Paul, Claiming Power*. Oxford University Press, 2014.

Schlesinger Library of American Women's History, Harvard.

Stevens, Doris. *Jailed for Freedom*. New York: Boni and Liveright, 1920, p. 356.